CHART PATTERNS FOR DAY TRADING

Candlestick chart Patterns,

Multiple Time Frames, Indicators For Intraday
Trading, Risk Managment

Green Ambi

This book CHART PATTERNS FOR DAY TRADING is committed to each forex, crypto dealer and furthermore for fledgling brokers and amateurs who are keen on learning and trading the forex market including old merchants too with almost no experience, taking the necessary steps to win in forex trading, rather than giving reasons.

Table of Content

Introduction

When you stare at candlestick charts and day trading patterns all day, do your eyes get watery?

Do those patterns on day trading charts seem more like a foreign language than a means of generating income?

I've been there, so I know.

I thought technical analysis was a type of stock astrology when I first started day trading and learned to read charts. But for me, everything changed when I learned how to read stock charts for day trading.

In this post, I'll demonstrate how to spot the best candlestick patterns on charts for day trading.

Whether you're looking at one-, five-, or fifteen-minute timeframes, there are significant day trading chart patterns that can help you identify opportunities to buy and

marketplace.

The importance of day trading charts, which charts to use, and how to incorporate them into your own trading charts are all covered in this article.

You will be able to identify every pattern on charts as a potential trade signal rather than just a disconnected set of lines at the end of this lesson.

You will see patterns such as the head and shoulders, ascending triangle, and shooting star. Understanding these patterns is like to following a daily trading road map.

Definition of Day Trading

Buying and selling securities within the same trading day, with all positions closed out prior to the market closure, is known as day trading.

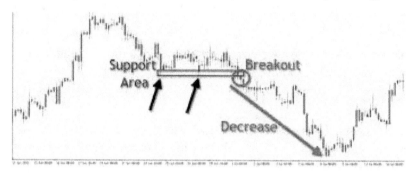

Day traders are active participants in the market who constantly keep an eye on stock prices and look for opportunities to profit swiftly from transient price swings.

The goal is to enter and exit trades in a matter of minutes or hours in order to profit from minute intraday price swings.

Although leverage and short sales can boost profits, day traders need to practice rigorous risk management to protect their gains from volatility.

Because technical analysis is crucial for spotting trades and planning entry and exit, day traders rely on it.

To identify momentum, support and resistance, and potential breakouts, one can use technical indicators, stock chart patterns, and other tools.

Candlestick charts are especially useful for day traders to spot reversals and possible bull or bear control areas.

Despite Gaining proficiency with intraday patterns and daily stock charts requires practice, but doing so provides a systematic trading strategy.

How Day Trading Patterns Are Found

You'll be continuously examining the candlestick chart when day trading in order to spot recurring intraday chart patterns that may indicate trading opportunities. The following advice can help you identify trends in the charts:

To see the most vivid portrayal of price action, use candlestick charts. Quickly emerging candlestick patterns include hammers, dojis, and bullish and bearish engulfing patterns.

Take a look at the 1-, 5-, and 15-minute time intervals to identify intraday patterns. To view both little and large price movements, enlarge and decrease the image.

Look for recurring candlestick patterns such as wedge patterns, channels, double tops/bottoms, triangles, flags, and head and shoulders during day trading.

Seek out places of resistance and support as these mimic pricing Where reversals frequently happen, price the ceilings and floors.

Take note of momentum patterns, such as upward trends with higher highs and lower lows or downward trends with lower highs and lower lows.

Watch for volume spikes, as they may be signs of major institutions taking positions or withdrawing from them.

For easy access, use chart pattern cheat sheets. As you continue to study charts, these patterns will become more apparent to you.

Trust signals for higher probability trades that coincide with several indicators or patterns.

You can identify common day trade patterns more quickly if you have this PDF of candlestick chart patterns for day trading close at hand.

Currently that After going over the basics, let's look at some particular guidelines to follow if you want to learn how to read day trading charts.

How to Read Chart Patterns Like a Pro

Follow these steps to read stock charts like a professional:

Identify the Trend Using Trend Lines

Look at the overall day trading chart to spot the dominant trend and draw trend lines connecting swing highs and swing lows:

Upward sloping trend lines show an uptrend.

Downward sloping lines indicate a downtrend.

Spot Consolidation Patterns

Notice areas where price consolidates into a tight range before continuing the trend. Common consolidation patterns include flags, triangles, rectangles, wedges. These form chart patterns on the day trading chart that offer easy breakout trades.

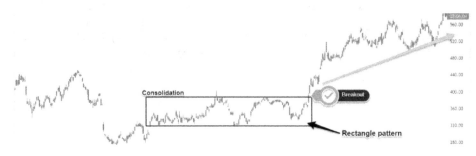

Watch for Reversal Patterns

Keep an eye out for reversal patterns signaling a potential trend reversal. Double tops, head and shoulders, and triple tops show upside resistance.

Analyze Candlestick Signals

Use candlestick charts for reversal signals:

A long upper wick reflects selling pressure

While a small body shows indecision.

A hammer candle reversal has a small body with long lower tail.

Hammer candlestick → ← Long lower wick and samll upper body

Trade the Momentum

After a downtrend, the first green candle closing above resistance indicates an upside entry. Capitalize on the momentum upwards after seeing this signal on the stock charts.

Volume should also validate the price move:

Heavy volume on breakouts confirms a robust move,

While light volume shows lack of commitment.

Use Multiple Time Frames

Zoom in and out on the day trading chart to identify the overall trend and potential entry points. 5-minute, 15-minute charts are great for entries.

Top Common Day Trading Patterns

These are some of the best chart patterns for day trading, get to know them:

Bearish and Bullish Engulfing

The engulfing pattern appears when a large real body candle fully engulfs the previous candle's body:

The bearish engulfing forms when a red down candle consumes the prior green candle.

The bullish version happens when an up green candle engulfs a preceding down red candle.

Both show a strong reversal signal.

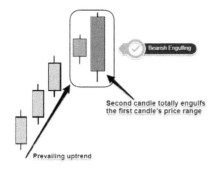

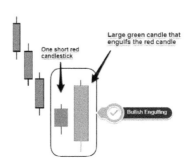

Head and Shoulders

The head and shoulders reversal pattern has a central peak (head) flanked by two smaller peaks (shoulders) with a neckline connecting the bottoms of the troughs. A breakdown below the neckline signals the trend may reverse at the right shoulder.

This pattern marks a potential trend exhaustion turning point.

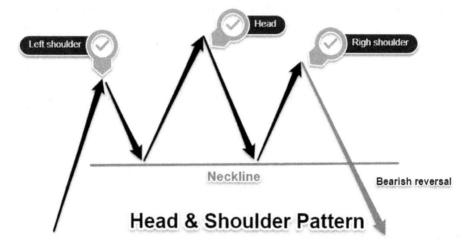

Head & Shoulder Pattern

Double Tops and Double Bottoms

Double tops and double bottoms are reversal patterns that signal a downtrend (uptrend) may be starting. Price tests support or resistance two times, showing buying demand or supply around those levels. After the final bounce off support (resistance), the turnaround upward breakout triggers entry.

Shooting Star and Morning Star

The shooting star is a 3-candle pattern signaling a potential trend reversal. It starts with a strong upward candle, followed by a small real body candle with a long upper wick indicating rejection of higher prices. The third candle closes lower, confirming the reversal.

The morning star is the opposite of the shooting star pattern.

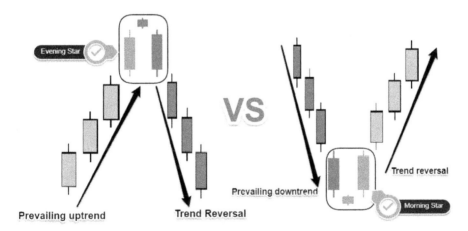

Hammer Candlestick

The hammer candle has a small real body near the top of its range with a long lower shadow demonstrating rejection of lower prices. Hammers are important chart patterns for day trading that indicate the downtrend may be ending soon and an upside reversal could follow.

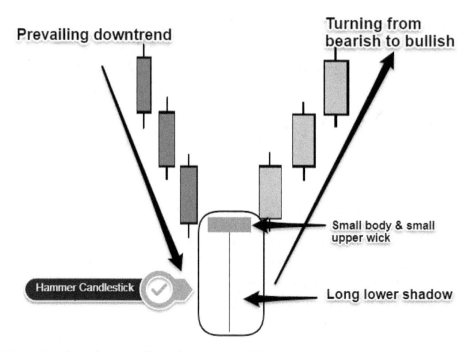

Mastering these key candlestick patterns will improve your trading but you need to combine them with other indicators like moving averages for higher probability setups.

Which Chart Pattern Is Best For Day Trading

The truth is that there isn't a single best chart pattern for day trading. Remaining adaptive and fluid, successful day traders are able to identify high-probability setups across a wide range of day trading candlestick patterns.

Nevertheless, in specific typical intraday circumstances, certain trade chart patterns do have a tendency to perform well:

Wedges, pennants, and flags are good continuation patterns to use when trading momentum-driven trends.

Dependable reversal patterns at support levels include double bottoms and inverse heads and shoulders.

Breakouts: When the price breaks above resistance following consolidation, these are clear entry.

Gaps: Openings above or below the previous close suggest that the market is moving quickly.

Let's now examine which time frames and day trading graphs offer the best intraday context balancing.

What Is the Best Chart Interval for Day Trading

Experienced day traders most commonly utilize:

15-minute charts - The 15-minute time frame is ideal for tracking overall intraday swings, support/resistance and momentum. The 15-minute chart for day trading provides a broad context.

5-minute - For nearer-term price action and entry timing, the 5-minute is ideal. Traders will zoom in to 5-minute day trading graphs to pinpoint trade location relative to key levels.

1-minute - Very short-term scalpers may go down to the 1-minute for extremely tight entries and exits. However, false signals are more common on the 1-minute interval.

In general, actively trading the 5-minute chart while referencing the 15-minute time frame for broader context offers an optimal balance but make sure to always confirm signals across multiple time frames.

The Top Pattern-Based Trading Strategies for Intraday

Pattern-based methods can offer structure for traders who are active and want to take advantage of short-term opportunities.

Which patterns in intraday stock trading offer consistent opportunities?

The top pattern-based strategies for intraday trading include the following:

Trading pullbacks inside established trends by purchasing dips in upward trends or selling rallies in downward trends is known as momentum continuation. Continuation patterns such as pennants and flags are effective.

Trading ranges on intraday charts are formed by distinct levels of support and resistance. Sell close to resistance and buy near support.

Trading against momentum when high-probability reversal patterns, such as double bottoms, appear near support or resistance is known as reversal trading.

Trade breakouts occur when a stock trade breaks above or below support following a phase of consolidation.

Trading gaps: When prices move noticeably above or below the close of the previous day, fade the gaps.

The optimal trading patterns to employ will vary based on the state of the market, so stay adaptable and concentrate on high probability setups with clearly defined risk/reward ratios.

Patterns on Common Day Trading Charts

Now that you understand reversal patterns, let's look at some typical chart patterns that might assist you in spotting possible market movements:

Symmetrical Triangle

Ascending Triangle

When price hits a resistance level and holds, the security's support continues to rise, as shown by the price producing higher lows (HL). Ascending triangles are formed in an uptrend.

The pattern is eventually continued when a buy imbalance develops and the price breaks out higher.

Descending Triangle

Descending triangles form in a downtrend when price reaches a support level that holds yet resistance is falling represented by price forming lower highs (LH).

Eventually a sell imbalance forms and price breaks out to the downside continuing the trend.

Symmetrical Triangle

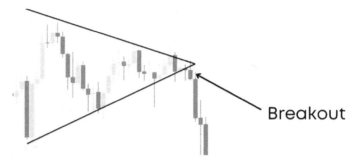

Finally, we have the symmetrical triangle pattern. Yep, just another fancy way to describe a pennant.

Price is trading into a constricting range and eventually an imbalance forms causing price to break out.

You can use these patterns on longer time frames to build context, or on your trigger charts to actually find entries.

Structural Trading Patterns

Structural trading patterns are defined by their shape, not as a result of consolidation.

While consolidation patterns can be used as a trigger or to build context, structural patterns are primarily used to build context around your setups.

1. Double Tops & Double Bottoms

Double tops and bottoms are great for building context and finding opportunities to look for a setup.

As the names imply, price retests a prior high or low and is rejected.

Double Bottom

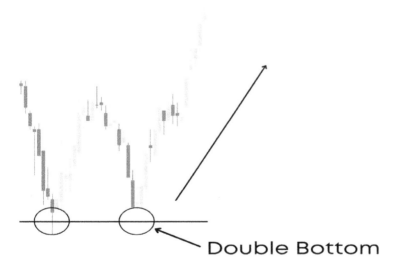

Double bottoms form after price is rejected for a second time at a support level, indicting a potential reversal in price.

This information is valuable for two reasons. First, it indicates a potential reversal. Second, it's provides you with a logical spot to place your stop loss order, below the swing low.

Double tops form after price is rejected for a second time at a resistance level, indicting a potential reversal in price.

You can also have triple or quadruple tops and bottoms, simply more confirmation of a support or resistance level.

2. Channels

Channels form in slower developing uptrends and downtrends. Recognizing when price is trading in a channel can be very useful to find setups with a high potential R.

Bullish Channel

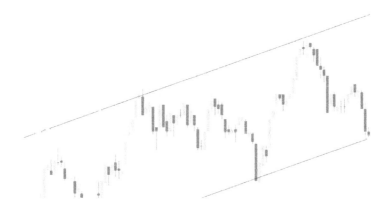

Bearish Channel

3. Head and Shoulders

Whoever came up with the name of this pattern deserves an award.

Head and shoulder patterns form at the end of trend, signaling a potential reversal.

They have four components: 2 Shoulders, a Head, and a Neckline.

Bullish Head & Shoulders

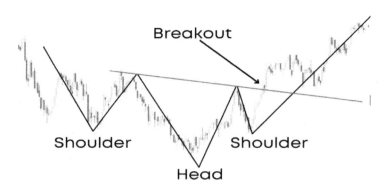

The four components are outlined in the bullish head and shoulders example above.

You would look to enter on the break of the neckline which is simply a trend line draw from the previous two highs.

A bullish head and shoulders pattern is nothing more than a price rejection on a retest of lows. So don't over think it.

Bearish Head & Shoulders

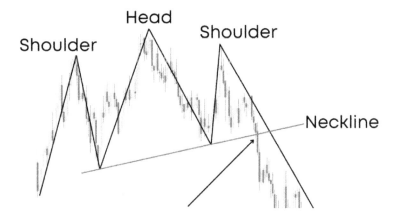

Above we have a bearish head and shoulders example. Notice how the right shoulder is simply a failed retest of highs. Entry would be on a break below the trendline (neckline).

4. Cup & Handle

The Cup & Handle pattern was first defined by swing traders a long time ago.

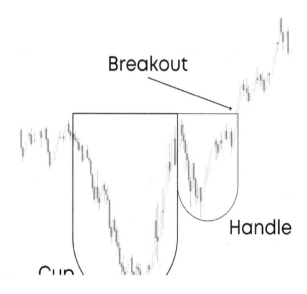

Cup and Handle patterns are easy to recognize by their large "U" shaped retracement followed by a smaller retracement where price fails to break lows.

When trading a cup and handle you look to enter on the break out of the handle and place your stop below the bottom of the handle.

5. ABCD Patterns

The final structural patterns we will look at are ABCD patterns.

ABCD patterns were founded by Gartley and are considered harmonic patterns. They're a great tool to help you manage your positions.

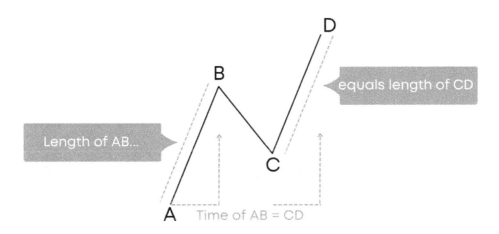

As the example above shows, an ABCD pattern with a standard configuration will have an AB leg that is equal to the CD leg in terms of price and time.

Once more, this is only an example. Not every time do the AB and CD legs take the same amount of time to finish?

Let's examine a few instances.

Bullish ABCD Pattern

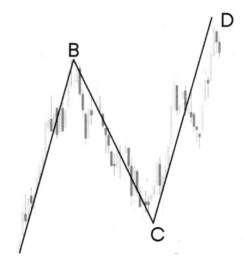

In the above bullish ABCD pattern, had you gone long near point C you would have targeted point D for your take profit.

Bearish ABCD Pattern

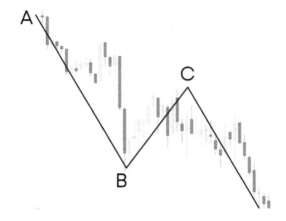

Similar to the bullish ABCD pattern, had you gone short at point C you would have targeted point D for your take profit.

To draw ABCD patterns on your charts, most platforms will have a Fibonacci Extension tool.

Finally, let's take a look at a few of my favorite candlestick patterns.

Candlestick Trading Patterns

Candlestick charts can trace their roots all the way back to the 18th century and Japanese rice traders.

The following patterns are very simple, yet can be extremely powerful when the proper context is applied.

1. Pin Bars

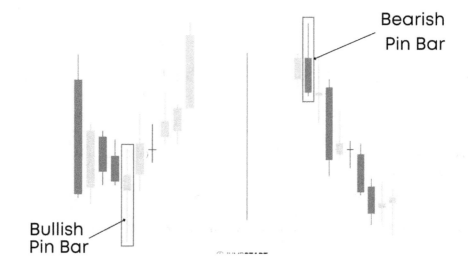

A pin bar is a single candlestick with a long tail (wick) who's price action demonstrates a rejection of a price level and reversal in price closing near its high (bullish pin bar) or low (bearish pin bar) for a user defined session.

They're great reversal patterns to include in your playbook. If you have interest in learning more about pin bars, I've written entire guide you can read here

2. Inverted Pin Bars

Inverted pin bars are single candlestick reversal patterns that typically have the potential for a high R due to their tight stop loss.

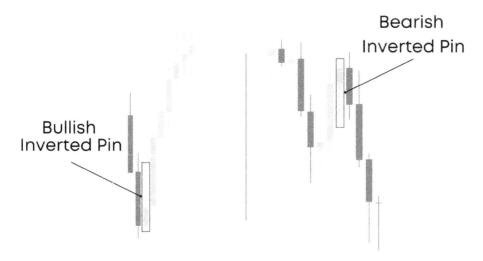

A pin bar is a single candlestick with a long tail (wick) who's price action demonstrates a rejection of a price level and reversal in price closing near its high (bullish pin bar) or low (bearish pin bar) for a user defined session.

They're great reversal patterns to include in your playbook. If you have interest in learning more about pin bars, I've written entire guide you can read here.

As may be observed on the left in the illustration above, bullish inverted pin bars appear during a decline.

The session began with buyers in control, but sellers quickly took the initiative and drove prices back toward lows. But sellers are unable to end the session at fresh lows, which suggests a possible turnaround is about to occur.

Because they provide you the ability to make an extremely tight halt just below the swing, inverted pins present high R possibilities.

You can notice their strength when you practice identifying them on your charts.

IPs can be used as a context off a longer interval or as a trigger.

3. Wicks

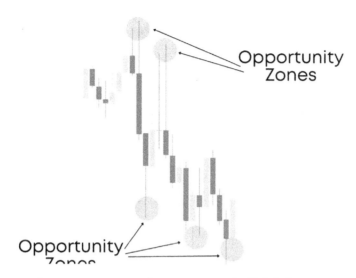

Wicks are another great pattern where you can find high R setups.

A large wick on a candlestick illustrates a fast rejection of price level, signaling capitulation and a potential reversal.

Personally I use wicks on a longer interval context chart to find potential areas to get long or short (opportunity zones). Let's look at an example.

On the right is a 15 minute chart of the e-Mini Nasdaq 100, and on the left a 1 minute chart.

The 1 minute chart is our trigger chart where we will look for an entry. The 15 minute chart we will use to build context and find a logical place to take an entry.

After the wick formed on the 15 minute chart, we define the extreme price zone of the wick as an opportunity zone. Why? Well we will assume that if price retraces back to the extreme of the wick that formed, that buyers will once again be the aggressor at those price levels.

We wait for a price retracement look for a setup. In this example an inverted pin bar forms which could have been you're trigger to go long.

How to Use Trading Patterns

It's very important you don't run just run off now and start trading the patterns you just learned on a live account.

Far too often I see new traders attempting to trade strategies with loose definitions and missing some of the key components that every trading strategy MUST HAVE.

Loose definitions lead to strategies that aren't repeatable, and red trading accounts.

Trading Strategy

1. Context
- Double Bottoms & Tops
- VWAP Retraces

2. Patterns (Triggers)
- Pin Bars
- Consolidation Breakouts

3. Trade Management
- Initial SL behind closest swing
- Trail swings, close half @ TP1

4. Risk Management
- 1% max per trade
- 3% max per day

A Trading Strategy is made up of four primary components: Context, Patterns (Triggers), Trade Management, & Risk Management.

Multiple Time Frame Analysis: What Is It?

The process of tracking and analyzing a certain currency pair in the Forex market over a variety of time periods and frequencies is known as multiple time frame analysis.

It assists traders in verifying price forecasts, market trends, and the best times to enter and exit the market. Your trading objectives and approach will determine how many and which frequencies you should watch; there are no hard-and-fast rules.

Advantage of multiple time frame analysis

1. By tracking the values of currency pairs over an extended period of time, Multiple Time Frame Analysis allows you to identify the market's crucial support and resistance levels.

Long-term market analysis provides you with the market's direction and trend, which enables you to make accurate predictions about future market movement.

As a trader, you can make more profitable transactions by following the market's direction or going against it, depending on what the support and resistance levels on the chart indicate.

In a downtrend, support levels indicate that traders should enter the market.

When the market is rising, resistance levels indicate that traders should sell.

2. Recognizes patterns in market prices

The market patterns show up differently throughout different time periods. For instance, when viewed over an extended period of time, a trend that appears to be going downward in the near term may actually be upward.

Therefore, traders can eliminate the possibility of false signals and identify the real market trends by employing many time frames when trading. Consequently, this leads to the placement of profitable trades in the market.

3. Offers points of entry and departure

Finding the best times to enter and exit the market is aided by trading with multiple time frame research. One of the main advantages of using multiple time frame analysis in trading is that it produces precise and lucrative trade decisions.

Which timeframes to use?

When beginning multi-timeframe trading, the first question that always arises is which periods to employ. I advise keeping it basic, particularly at first, and restricting it to the two timeframes you utilize for trading.

The fact that novice traders typically trade the improper time frame for their personalities is one of the reasons they don't perform as well as they should.

New forex traders will begin trading short time frames, such as 1- or 5-minute charts, since they want to make money fast.

Because the time constraint doesn't suit their personalities, they eventually become frustrated when trading.

The 1-hour charts are the most comfortable for certain forex traders.

There are fewer trading indications, but not too few, and the time frame is longer, but not too long.

This time limit for trading allows us more time to study the market and avoid feeling hurried.

Trading the incorrect time frame for their personality is one of the reasons novice traders don't perform as well as they ought to.

In an attempt to make rapid money, novice forex traders will begin trading on short time frames, such as 1- or 5-minute charts.

When they trade, they eventually become dissatisfied because the time frame doesn't suit their personalities.

The 1-hour charts are where some forex traders feel most at ease.Trade signals are fewer but not excessively so, and the time frame is longer but not too so.

Trading throughout this period of time allows one to take their time and not feel hurried.

Because actual money is at stake in a trade, you will always experience some level of pressure or frustration.

It's normal.

However, you shouldn't believe that the strain is due to things moving too quickly for you to make decisions or too slowly for you to become impatient.

We were unable to adhere to a schedule when we first started trading.

Test a Variety of Time Frames

First, we looked at the 15-minute chart.

The 5-minute chart follows.

Next, we experimented with the 1-hour, daily, and 4-hour charts.

This is normal for all novice forex traders until they find their comfort zone,

which is why we advise you to DEMO trade across a variety of time periods to determine which best suits your personality.

The best timeframes for day traders in FX

Most day traders choose timeframes ranging from 15 minutes to four hours, indicating that they often choose a short-term strategy.

Being a day trader has the advantage of allowing you to select from a variety of timeframes based on your preferred trading technique, the liquidity of the market you have selected, and the amount of time you have to make deals.

For example, a forex trader with limited time may utilize a 15-minute timeframe to generate rapid profits in a liquid market within a condensed period of time.

To spot new trends and choose the ideal timing to enter the market, a full-time day trader may employ hourly and daily timeframe research.

Day traders must, however, exercise caution when setting tight exit points after entering the market of their choice and keep a close eye on these price swings. A single bad trade might wipe out all of the profits from an entire day.

The best timeframes for swing traders in forex

Because they may analyze price trends and patterns over time, swing traders typically select longer horizons. These timelines

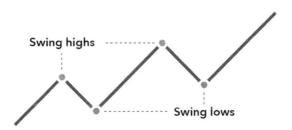

Swing trading is based on the idea that by keeping an eye on macrotrends and employing technical analysis to determine the optimal entry points, one can profit from overall price movement over time.

This approach, which is most effective with less volatile currency pairs, rewards perseverance and market knowledge.

The best timeframes for position traders in forex

Position traders, as the name implies, will take a position in a specific forex market and hold it with the expectation that its value would rise over a given time frame.

These traders are likely to operate over very lengthy timeframes, such as weeks, months, or even a year, and they won't actually make many deals.

Position traders do not only lock their money away indefinitely, in contrast to conventional "buy and hold" investors. As trend followers, their objective is to spot a trend, invest in it, and then sell out when it peaks.

How to conduct analysis across several timeframes

The goal of multiple timeframe analysis is to identify as many trading opportunities as possible by simultaneously examining a specific currency pair over a number of distinct time periods.

The majority of traders will begin by selecting two timeframes: one longer and one shorter. When using multiple timeframe analysis, traders typically utilize a ratio of 1:4 or 1:6, with a one-hour chart serving as the lower timeframe and a four- or six-hour chart as the longer timeframe.

While the shorter duration can be utilized to determine the best times to enter the market, the longer timeframe can be used to develop a trend. After that, a third, medium-term timeframe can be included to enable more detailed study.

You can manage multiple trading positions at once without raising your risks by using multiple timeframe analysis approaches. This trading technique can potentially benefit from the usage of indicators.

Multi-timeframe strategies

After deciding on a period combination, we examine the combined utilization of the upper and lower timeframes.

You must first clearly define your higher timetable and what you are especially seeking for.

Here, traders have a wide range of higher timeframe "cues" (also known as confluence factors) to pick from.

For your own multi-timeframe strategy, you can select the appropriate signals based on your preferred chart analysis methodology.

Trading Indicators for Various Timeframes

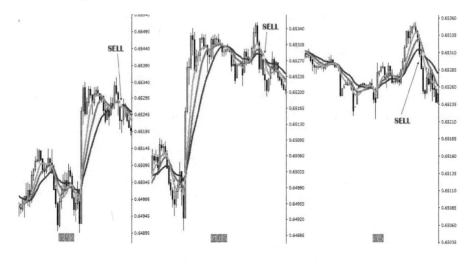

Selecting the best timeframe combination is way to of success in the future. Finding the precise entry and exit sites is crucial. An example based on the idea of resistance and support was examined above.

But indication analysis is the most widely used technique. This approach allows traders to employ a variety of technical indicators, ranging from simple moving averages to intricate oscillators like the RSI, CCI, and stochastic.

Using the fundamental configuration of three exponential moving averages (EMA), the accompanying figure illustrates trading on the M30, M15, and M5 time frames. The following outlines the strategy's working principle:

Use three Moving Average indicators on three time frames with the following basic parameters: 21, 13, and 8. In blue, indicate the slowest, the The quickest is in green, and the average is in red.

The first indication will be blue. A transaction will be opened once the other two have broken it out.

On each of the three timeframes, wait for two fast EMAs to cross the signal one.

It is a buy indication when it crosses from bottom to top, and a sell signal when it crosses from top to bottom. This is a sell signal for us.

Open a sell trade as soon as you get the signal.

You must evaluate the market conditions from top to bottom and take into account a number of charts and timeframes in order to decide when to enter the market. In other words, from the longest to the shortest time period.

It will just take a few minutes to identify market entry and trends. Opening a trade is a solid idea if the current trend is moving in the same direction across all three time frames. When the trend reverses, especially if all three charts support it, that is when the trades will be most profitable.

Identify the Primary Trend

Determine the main trend (developing over two to three days) on the longest time period we are taking into consideration first. Keep in mind that the macro trend is only visible over an extended period of time.

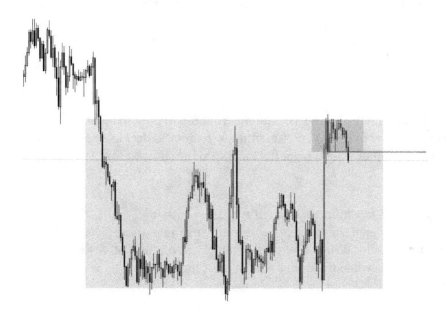

Chart shows two main trends, downward and sideways. The downtrend is global and has been developing for a long time. Let's study the sideways trend. The good thing about it is that it is easy to determine its borders (support and resistance lines).

Traders should start trading from these lines. So, the main trend is flat. The price is located at its upper border. In this situation, the price can either break out the resistance line and go up, breaking the trend, or reverse and continue the trend. It is the reversal that is most interesting, since it supports the current trend, which means such a trade is the safest.

Determine Current Market Bias

The next timeframe tells us the medium-term bias; if the global one displays a trend of two to three days, then the current one reveals changes within the day. Rule 2: Determine Current Market Bias Next, you must ascertain the current trend.

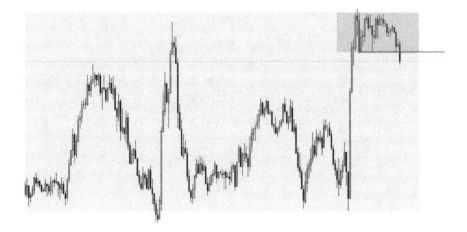

The direction of the intraday movement is confirmed by the present trend on the lower time frame. At the resistance line, the chart confirms a potential reversal.

The price has already surpassed the daily trend's lows and is making an effort to leave the local sideways channel. There aren't many differences between the 30M and 15M timeframes, and the candles on them will typically be the same color.

By comparing the color of the most recent candles on various periods, traders can rapidly identify the trend while trading on three timeframes using a candlestick chart.

The final black candles on M30 and M15 indicate that the trend direction is the same. The M15 thus validates in full the

Determine Entry and Exit

Use short-term charts to determine the best times to enter and exit a trade after the current trend has been verified. The similar colors of the previous candles on all three periods, along with a trend reversal, will indicate an entry into the market. This is a split of the local channel support line in our situation.

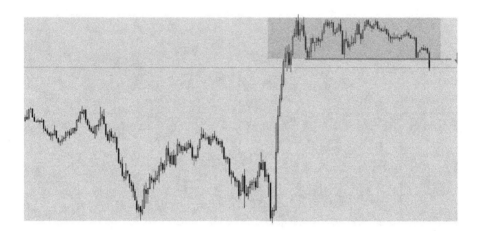

Since large time frames do not offer the required price accuracy, it is preferable to enter a trade on the lowest time frame. You can initiate a sell trade once all confirmations have been received.

Using risk management guidelines, pinpoint the precise entry and exit points. As soon as the signal is confirmed, a sell transaction can be initiated; it is preferable to exit the trade at the take-profit level.

Setting it around the global channel's support line on the M30 period makes sense in this case. Setting the stop loss level above the global channel's resistance line is preferable.

Three Forex Market Timeframes for Trading

Modern technical analysis offers a wide variety of tactics, and traders occasionally overlook the fact that the most straightforward ones are the most successful. Three time frame trading is a potent trading technique that enables traders to turn a profit with little time commitment.

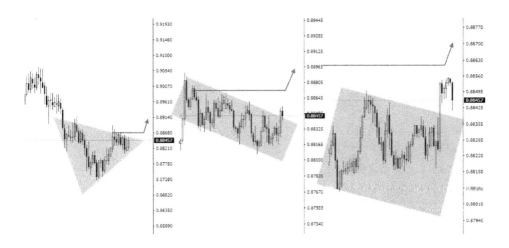

Three timeframes for trading are separated into:

long-range. The typical exchange lasts more than a week or perhaps a month.

in the middle term. The deal lasts anything from a few days to a week.

brief. Shorter periods are used by traders to open deals without waiting for the next day.

The daily chart is the most often used time period since it enables traders to make thoughtful trading decisions. It is easier to concentrate on trading management when the timeframe is longer.

The trade is more secure the more time you have. The daily chart also makes it easy to see all of the prominent trends.

Use the following three guidelines when trading three time frames:

Avoid trading against the world's trend.

Only enter trades if the color of the last three timeframes' candles is the same.

If market volatility is excessive, avoid opening deals.

Intraday Trading Indicators:

In order to analyze and forecast market behavior within a single trading day, traders rely heavily on intraday trading indicators. These indicators assist traders in determining possible reversal points, market momentum, and price patterns.

Through the interpretation of these signals, traders can maximize their earnings and minimize their risks by making well-informed judgments regarding whether to enter or exit a trade.

The Exponential Moving Average (EMA), which smoothes out price data to make trends easier to see, the Relative Strength Index (RSI), which signals

overbought or oversold circumstances, and Bollinger Bands, which gauge market volatility, are common intraday trading indicators. When combined, the distinct insights from each indicator offer a thorough understanding of market movements, assisting traders in navigating the rapidly change in the world of intraday trading.

Importance of Intraday Indicator

Because they provide instantaneous insights into the short-term swings of the stock market, intraday indicators are essential. Intraday trading necessitates prompt decision-making, in contrast to long-term trading, and these indicators assist traders in determining possible entry and exit positions within a single trading day.

Real-time Analysis: Intraday indicators give traders the most recent information on price movements, allowing them to respond quickly to shifts in the market.

Trend Identification: By assisting in the identification of market trends, these indicators enable traders to follow rather than deviate from the market's direction.

Risk management: To reduce possible losses and lock in winnings, traders can use indicators to determine take-profit and stop-loss levels.

Enhanced Accuracy: By combining several indicators, traders can increase prediction accuracy and make better-informed choices.

Enhanced Accuracy: By combining several indicators, traders can increase prediction accuracy and make better-informed choices.

List of Technical Indicators for Trading

1. Convergence of Moving Averages Divergence (MACD)

Goal: A trend-following and momentum indicator that illustrates the correlation between two moving averages of the price of a securities.

Parts: consists of the signal line (9-day MACD EMA), the MACD line (difference between a 12-day and 26-day EMA), and the histogram (difference between the MACD line and signal line).

Use: As buy/sell signals, traders watch for crossovers between the MACD and the signal line.

2. The ADX, or Average Directional Index

Goal: Indicates a trend's strength rather than its direction. From 0 to 100 is the range. A strong trend is often indicated by a value above 25, whilst a weak trend is shown by a value below 20.

Use: To ascertain if the market is trending or range-bound, it is combined with other indicators.

3. The RSI, or Relative Strength Index

Its purpose is to measure the speed and change of price fluctuations using a momentum oscillator.

Overbought levels are over 70 and oversold levels are below 30 in the range of 0 to 100.

Use: Indicates overbought or oversold circumstances to spot possible reversals.

Top Technical Indicators for Intraday Trading

Maximizing success in hectic trading settings requires an understanding of the top technical intraday trading indicators. The most useful indicators for intraday traders are examined below, along with real-world examples and uses.

1. The Bollinger Bands

John Bollinger developed the popular technical analysis tool known as Bollinger Bands. A 20-day simple moving average (SMA) makes up the middle

band; an upper band is set at +2 standard deviations from the SMA; and a lower band is set at -2 standard deviations from the SMA. These bands show how volatile a stock's price is. The bands expand in periods of high market volatility and compress in periods of low volatility.

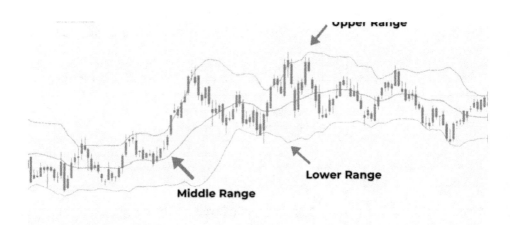

Bollinger Bands are used by intraday traders to determine the volatility and price range of stocks. The stock price may be overbought, indicating a possible sell opportunity, when it touches the upper band. On the other hand, a possible buy opportunity is indicated when the stock price approaches the lower band, suggesting that the stock may be oversold. Traders can find possible entry and exit points by observing the constant movement of stock prices between the upper and lower bands.

2. The RSI, or Relative Strength Index

One of the greatest technical indicators is the Relative Strength Index (RSI), a momentum oscillator that gauges the rate and direction of price changes. It was created by J. Welles Wilder and goes from 0 to 100.

It assists traders in determining when the market is overbought and oversold. Generally speaking, an RSI value above 70 suggests that a stock is overbought and may be a sell indication, whilst a value below 30 suggests that a stock is oversold and may be a buy signal.

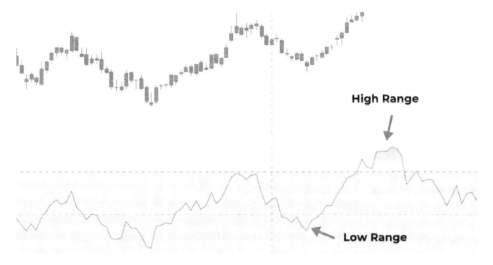

3. The EMA, or exponential moving average

One kind of moving average that gives more weight and importance to the most recent data points is the Exponential Moving Average (EMA).

The EMA responds to recent price movements faster than the Simple Moving Average (SMA), which gives each data point equal weight. Because of this, it is a well-liked tool for intraday traders who want accurate alerts.

Trends and possible reversal points are found using EMAs. For example, a bullish trend and a potential purchasing opportunity may be indicated when a shorter-term EMA crosses above a longer-term EMA.

On the other hand, a bearish trend and a potential selling opportunity may be indicated when a shorter-term EMA crosses below a longer-term EMA. Intraday traders can enhance their timing for entering and leaving trades and gain a better understanding of market direction by utilizing EMAs.

4. Convergence Divergence of Moving Averages (MACD)

One of the most widely utilized momentum indicators in technical analysis is the Moving Average Convergence Divergence (MACD). It displays the correlation between two stock price moving averages.

The 26-day Exponential Moving Average (EMA) is subtracted from the 12-day EMA to determine the MACD. The MACD line is the outcome. The MACD line, which can serve as a trigger for buy and sell signals, is then plotted over a nine-day EMA of the MACD known as the signal line.

The MACD assists intraday traders in recognizing shifts in a trend's strength, direction, momentum, and longevity. It may be a good opportunity to buy when the MACD line crosses above the signal line, indicating a bullish indication.

On the other hand, a bearish signal that suggests a potential selling opportunity is indicated when the MACD line crosses below the signal line. Because it allows traders to identify possible entry and exit positions based on changes in momentum, the MACD is especially helpful in trending markets.

5. SAR that is parabolic

One technical indicator for determining the direction of an asset's momentum and possible reversal points is the Parabolic SAR (Stop and Reverse).

A sequence of dots above or below the price chart represents it; an upward trend is indicated by dots above, while a downward trend is indicated by dots below. The dots go closer to the price as the trend continues, and when they cross over, it could indicate a possible reversal.

Intraday traders set trailing stop-loss orders using the Parabolic SAR. With this approach, they can lock in winnings when the price rises in their favor because the stop-loss level is dynamically adjusted.

The Parabolic SAR helps traders stay in lucrative trades longer and exit at the best times, making it particularly helpful in trending markets.

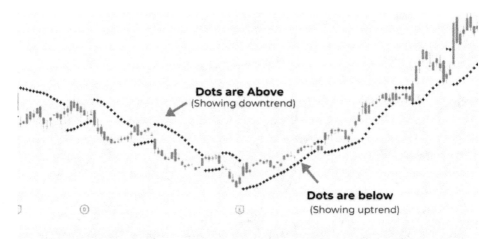

You can see how the trend's direction is indicated by the Parabolic SAR dots in this graphic. The dots lie below the price during an uptrend, indicating to traders that they should keep or start long bets.

The dots get closer as the price increases, creating a trailing stop level. The dots shift to above the price when the trend reverses, alerting traders to either consider short bets or leave long positions.

6. Turning Points

Intraday traders employ pivot points, a well-liked technical analysis indicator, to identify possible market support and resistance levels. The high, low, and closing prices from the previous day are used to determine these levels. Pivot points are a useful tool for traders to use when identifying market trends and possible reversal points.

making them a useful instrument for trading decision-making. The average of the preceding trading day's high, low, and close is the main pivot point. To give a thorough picture of the possible price changes in the market, other support and resistance levels are derived from this fundamental pivot point.

Traders plot these levels on their charts and search for price interactions with pivot points in order to use them successfully. For example, a bullish feeling and possible purchasing opportunities are indicated if the price is trading above the major Pivot Point.

On the other hand, pessimistic sentiment and possible selling opportunities are indicated if the price is below the pivot point. Pivot points are frequently used by traders in conjunction with other technical indicators, including as volume and moving averages, to support their trading plans and improve their decision-making. The chart that follows shows pivot points together with the levels of support and resistance for each:

The main Pivot Point, support (S1, S2), and resistance (R1, R2) levels are all indicated on this chart. Traders observe when the price gets closer to certain levels.

Information Offered by Intraday Indicators

Important information is provided by intraday indicators to assist traders in making prompt and well-informed decisions. They provide information about:

1. Market Trends: By displaying the general direction of the market, indicators such as trend lines and moving averages assist traders in adjusting their strategies to follow the current trend.

2. Volatility: Market volatility is measured by tools like Bollinger Bands and Average True Range (ATR), which assist traders control risk by pointing out possible price fluctuations.

3. Momentum: Price movements' strength and speed are measured by oscillators like the Moving Average Convergence Divergence (MACD) and Relative Strength Index (RSI), which indicate possible entry and exit positions.

4. Volume Analysis: Trading activity, price trends, and possible reversals are tracked by indicators such as volume and on-balance volume (OBV).

Tools for Technical Analysis in Trading

For intraday traders to evaluate market circumstances and make wise judgments, technical analysis tools are crucial. These resources support traders in analyzing price data, spotting patterns, and creating winning plans.

1. Charting Software: TradingView and MetaTrader are two platforms that give traders a clear picture of market trends by enabling them to visualize price movements, customize charts, and apply different indicators.

Premium TradingView charts, which enable several indicators on a single chart, are available through Lakshmishree.

2. Trend Lines: Using trend lines to guide entry and exit points on price charts, one may determine the market's direction, support, and resistance levels.

3. Support and Resistance: Support is the price at which a stock typically attracts purchasing interest, halting further declines. Resistance has a cost.

level at which a stock typically encounters selling interest, halting further growth.

4. Candlestick Patterns: By revealing information about market mood and possible reversals, patterns like doji and hammer aid traders in predicting price movements.

5. Fibonacci Retracement: This tool shows possible support and resistance levels where market corrections can take place by drawing horizontal lines at significant Fibonacci levels.

Volume Analysis

In stock trading, volume is a metric that quantifies the quantity of shares exchanged during a given period of time. It displays the time frame of the price bars for that particular period and is typically shown at the bottom of a trading chart.

A one-minute chart, for instance, will display the price's opening, peak, low, and close over the course of one minute. The total number of shares exchanged during that one-minute period is displayed in the related volume.

Volume analysis reveals buying or selling pressure, which helps validate breakouts, indicate possible reversals, and confirm trends.

Strong buying interest, for example, is indicated by a price increase on large volume, indicating that the trend is likely to continue.

A price rise on low volume, however, might not be as trustworthy!All assets can employ volume, but there are certain distinctions that I'll discuss later in this post.

Choose any chart by navigating to your Trading View panel.

The Indicators tab is located at the top of the chart.

The Significance of Volume

Volume indicates how many contracts or shares were exchanged during a specific period of time.

Increased trading activity and interest in the asset, frequently accompanied by significant price swings, are indicators of high volume.

Low volume might indicate times of consolidation or moderate price moves, as well as a lack of interest.

Volume analysis's primary objective is to assist you in making better judgments by highlighting the strength or weakness of price movements.

Instead of being the entry trigger itself, it is frequently utilized as confirmation.

Keep in mind that volume can be influenced by a variety of things, which I will discuss in more detail later in this post.

You may wonder why some of the bars are green and some are red.

Let's examine.

Red Bars against Green Bars

Traders frequently confuse the red and green hues for the volume itself.

They only indicate if the price increased or decreased at that time, though.

The volume bar will be green if the price has increased since the last candlestick.

The price will be red if it drops from the preceding candlestick.

These colors frequently have too much of an impact on traders' choices when, in reality, the height and variation of volume bars matter more!

There is one important thing you should know before delving into the specifics of using volume for charting.

It's critical to keep in mind that the volume of stocks and forex differs.

Furthermore, volume for stocks versus forex

In actuality, volume has long been seen to be far more significant for equities.

Here's why.

Volume Difference between Stocks and Forex

The structure of the stock and FX markets causes differences in volume analysis.

On controlled exchanges such as the NYSE or NASDAQ, where volume data is readily available and transparent, stocks are traded.

On the other hand, volume data in the decentralized FX market depends on the broker.

It implies that, when considering the market as a whole, the volume data in forex markets may not be entirely trustworthy.

Despite this, volume analysis is still useful in forex trading because the majority of major forex brokers provide comparable volume data that captures the mood of the market as a whole.

However, one aspect is that there may be additional difficulties when examining volume in forex at shorter timescales.

Although it can provide information about intraday trade activity and assist in identifying possible

What is the Typical Use of Volume?

You now understand the purpose of volume and where to locate it in Tradingview.

However, how may it be applied when examining a chart?

Never used alone; always used as confirmation in conjunction with a strategy.

Volume analysis should not be used alone, but rather in conjunction with other technical indicators and chart patterns.

It ought to act as a tool for confirming your trading techniques and indications.

By displaying the degree of market participation, volume analysis, for example, might validate the strength of a technical indicator that points to a possible transaction.

A successful deal is more likely when a large volume and a signal indicate considerable market interest.

The Average Volume in a Particular Area

I frequently witness traders make the error of focusing only on the volume of a single session rather than adopting a comprehensive strategy.

To determine the normal trading activity for a securities, I like to examine the average volume over a given time frame.

An impending big move may be indicated by an abrupt increase in volume above the average.

For instance, you might start paying more attention and constructing a case for buying a company if its average volume is rather flat but, for some reason, a few volume bars start to show higher volume at a value area.

Verification of Trend Continuation

Trend continuation can be verified using volume analysis.

Strong purchasing interest is shown by rising volume as the price rises in an uptrend, which suggests the trend is likely to continue.

Price charts also show that during an uptrend, there are frequently brief, tiny pullbacks.

It may indicate that the pullbacks are feeble and the uptrend is robust enough to last if the volume of the upward advances is high and that of the modest retracements is low.

Confirmation of Candlestick Volume

As you are aware if you have been following me for a while, I adore my candlestick designs!

Volume, however, can give them an additional layer.

A bullish engulfing pattern, for instance, that appears on large volume signals a strong reversal indication because it shows

because it shows a lot of interest in purchasing.

Your analysis would gain power from volume confirmation of candlestick patterns, which would enable you to forecast future price moves with more accuracy.

Confirmation of Breakout

When it comes to loudness, breakouts are also no exception.Crucial moments when the price shifts above or below resistance or support levels are known as breakouts.

Because high volume during a breakout indicates robust market activity and raises the possibility of a prolonged price movement, it can help validate that the breakout is legitimate.

On the other hand, low volume indicates insufficient market interest and a greater chance of a false breakout if the price breaks out of a range.

Traders can increase the efficacy of their trading techniques by determining which breakouts are real or fake by examining volume during breakouts.

You must understand how to view volume and VWAP on your trading platform in order to use them successfully.

This is a brief tutorial for TradingView:

To view volume, open your TradingView chart.

At the top of the screen, click the "Indicators" button.

Look up "Volume" and choose it. This will cause your chart's volume bars, which indicate how many shares were traded during each time period, to appear at the bottom.

To add VWAP, click the "Indicators" button once again.

Look up "VWAP" and choose it. Your chart will display the volume-weighted average price over the course of the trading session as the VWAP line.

Basic Analysis

Using indicators, fundamental analysis forecasts future price changes. This can be accomplished in a number ways, such as:

1. The method from the top down: This method starts with the economy as a whole before gradually delving into other sectors and businesses to assess their performance.

This entails assessing a nation's economic health (by looking at economic indicators) and attempting to ascertain the direction of the economy and how it will impact particular businesses and industries.

2. The bottom-up method: This method looks at individual businesses to determine which ones are worth investing in. It can be quite rewarding for an investor to just invest in a firm that is doing something good.

Even if it might not be the greatest industry to be in at the moment, this method finds businesses that are performing well in comparison to their sector and are therefore a decent investment.

Measures of the economy

Finding out if the news release will meet or exceed market expectations is the next stage in this process. Right now, it's critical to examine the neutral rate.

We may predict that a news release that is above the neutral rate will have a positive impact on the currency, whilst one that is below the neutral rate will have a negative impact.

Keep in mind that choosing an interest rate is not always as straightforward as deciding whether it will be beneficial or bad for the currency.

if lowered. Interest rate choices can have complex implications on currency because they are frequently influenced by other news items. Examining the changes made to earlier news releases is also crucial.

Could a news release influence current trends? We will have a better grasp of the potential market impact of the news release thanks to the responses to these questions.

News and earnings releases from the company

The greatest source of information for trading decisions is the company's news and earnings reports.

underlying analysis is the process by which a trader attempts to comprehend the value of a company's stock by examining the underlying financial elements that influence the company's worth, as opposed to technical analysis, which is based on price movements and patterns.

Fundamental analysis assumes that a stock's price will eventually move toward its true value, which is then reflected by events that will have a direct impact on the business, such as profits, a new product, and so forth.

Generally speaking, the trader's goal is to ascertain if the stock is overpriced or undervalued, and then base their trading decision on this determination.

While longer-term traders will just do what is best to bring the stock to fair value, the more short-term trader may try to enter a position just before a likely price move.

Since earnings reports are a crucial gauge of a company's profitability, they can cause unpredictable and swift fluctuations in the share price.

Analyst estimates and actual reported earnings are reviewed, and any differences—whether favorable or unfavorable—usually result in significant price changes as traders and investors reevaluate.

A currency will often benefit from a significant upward revision to a prior release, whereas a significant downward revision will be detrimental.

It's crucial to assess the significance of each news release before deciding to trade on it. The following inquiries should be kept in mind: In comparison to other news releases, is this one significant?

Will only one country or all of them be impacted by the news release? Will there be a short-term or long-term effect from the news release? Does the

the value of the business. Because some people expect a trend reversal and others expect enhanced momentum, an earnings surprise frequently sparks speculative activity.

One way to profit from this is to determine the stock price's expected future trend.

Analysis of the industry

A collection of businesses that are similar in their main lines of operation constitute an industry.

There is usually a lot of information and publicity on the market's large firms.

By improving the accessibility and dependability of information about the company and its short- and long-term commercial prospects, this can benefit day traders.

This improved information accessibility aids in reducing the range of results for individual stock investments, as the The stock price may be significantly influenced by the company's outlook.

Analysis of large-cap firms increases the likelihood of using techniques with positive expectations by reducing the trade's variation.

In contrast, smaller businesses or industries may offer more room for speculation, but they also have a greater chance of failing and a wider range of potential outcomes.

A day trader may be tempted to focus exclusively on companies in a certain industry due to the availability of high-quality data about those companies.

With careful planning, this can be transformed into a reliable trading technique.

A trader who finds a few consistently positive sectors and only trades the stocks of companies inside those sectors when the timing is right is an example.

the plan. Another trader may concentrate on shorting the stock of heavily indebted corporations in a collapsing industry.

These companies are at greater risk of poor future performance and a drop in stock price since they frequently have higher costs of capital and are under more pressure to repay loans.

A valuable source of long-term and short-term trading methods for a day trader is knowledge of industries and corporate positions.

Macroeconomic events have the potential to benefit one industry while harming another. One obvious example of a factor that can help or hurt businesses in various energy sectors is the price of oil on a global scale.

Short-term, well-publicized occasions like new product releases or court rulings can cause significant changes in a single company's stock price.

By predicting the event and adopting the right long or short position in advance, day traders who have a solid understanding of these factors can frequently make money.

Risk Management

The most important day trading tactic is the use of stop-loss orders. The fundamental idea is that a minor loss early on and capital preservation are preferable to a big loss later.

Stop-loss orders come in two varieties: normal and trailing. If the market hits a specific level, standard stops merely execute a sell order. Using the same reasoning as the 1% rule, a trailing stop will continue with the upward market trend.

More information on trading on margin will be included in the section on trading with leverage. A stop-loss order won't shield you from losses brought on by margin trading. Even if the market moves negatively, an investor might still have to repay the loan and possibly interest for the margin. Although it can be reduced by trading solely at 1:1 leverage and applying the 1% rule, this still poses a significant danger to the capital.

You may only make a certain number of deals every day using this day trading method, and you must be selective about which trades you make in order to succeed.

If you use the 1% rule on a £10,000 account, you are risking £100. If you trade with a stop-loss of 10 pip, you are risking £10 per pip, which is equivalent to a position of 1 lot.

The transactions with the greatest potential for profit and the least amount of cash are the best ones. Therefore, starting with the deals that carry the least amount of risk is the wisest course of action.

As capital increases, strive for the riskier deals. As a result, even though a highly leveraged trade will have a higher percentage of low-risk deals, an aggressive day trader can still join the market through variance.

This tactic gets ready for 4.2: Determining Position Size. An investor can still incur a 1% loss on capital by holding off on making the riskiest trades.

Traders can place typical stop-loss orders with decreasing risk until capital is conserved if a trade does not work out.

Putting stop-loss orders in place

An order filed with a broker to buy or sell a securities at a specific price is known as a stop-loss order.

The purpose of a stop-loss order is to restrict the amount of money that an investor can lose on a security holding.

Stop-loss orders can be used for both short and long positions in stocks, despite the fact that most investors only think of them in relation to long positions.

A stop-loss order specifies the following two prices: (1) Trigger price: The stop-loss order is activated and turns into a market order when this price is reached.

Market price: The market order is executed at this price. If the market is moving quickly, it can be the same as the trigger price or it might be different. Assume For $17, an investor purchases 100 shares of Ford Motor Company.

If the stock drops three points to $14, an investor may place a stop-loss order to sell. The trigger price is $14.

The investor's 100 shares will be sold at the best price on the market once the trigger price is achieved, turning the stop-loss order into a market order.

Determining the size of the position

where r is the expected opportunity cost (often set to 0), f* is the optimal fraction of Kelly, σ^2 is the expected variance of the transaction, and μ is the expected return.

Another mathematician, Kelly, developed a betting strategy that optimized the rate of capital growth. He stated that his aim was to maximize the anticipated log of riches.

Even though the preceding calculation provides the ideal Kelly fraction, using this much leverage is not advised; instead, a lesser fraction, like half Kelly or a quarter Kelly, is typically employed. Here's an illustration of how to apply this:

$$f^* = (\mu - r)/\sigma^2$$

Volatility is used in other techniques. The goal is to increase the size of the position when volatility rises and lower it when volatility falls.

Ralph Vince's book "The Handbook of Portfolio Mathematics" produced the most widely used form of this technique, known as the Optimal-f method. The following formula is used in this method:

In the trading community, the conventional approach to position sizing is the Fixed

The percentage approach. Here, you risk a specific proportion of your trading capital on each deal.

According to the hypothesis, if you risk, say, 2% on each trade, you will only lose 20% of your trading account if you have a losing streak of, say, 10 deals.Only 20% of your trading account will be deducted.

The capacity to manage risk and diversify by determining the position size for a given trade is one of the most important components of a successful trading strategy.

In trading, it's not uncommon for someone to have a few profitable trades followed by a significant loss. Losing deals are what cause you to lose money in trading, not winning ones.

Finding the position size that would optimize the growth of the trading account and determining the risk of ruin for a certain strategy are therefore crucial.

Portfolio management and diversification

It is difficult to determine how much diversification is sufficient, but it is extremely simple to recognize when it is excessive.

Each trader has a financial cap on how much time and energy they can devote to trading. Spreading that time too thin across too many positions makes no sense and makes the time spent managing the transactions and conducting research useless.

Since most short-term methods are unlikely to offer ten excellent trading opportunities every day, taking ten transactions every day may overstate the situation. Setting a minimum and maximum restriction on the number of trades one will make in a given period of time is quite helpful for traders.

day, considering the trading system in question. This can lessen the chance that a method with a high win rate will be overtraded or that legitimate trading chances will go unnoticed.

The difference between the trade's entry point and stop loss should represent the trader's realistically estimated effective risk.

This is not all of the trade's risk because, with rare exceptions, it is illogical to never move a stop loss to breakeven when there is a chance to lower risk.

However, the degree of risk associated with the opportunity is what distinguishes an entry from a halt. It need to serve as the foundation for the utmost effective risk standards for all positions.

It's really Some traders may find it easier to risk a predetermined proportion of their total capital on each trade, as it can be challenging to keep an eye on numerous positions to make sure the risk on each trade is adhering to the guidelines.

This approach is not advised because a percentage of capital risk can significantly increase position sizes after a winning period and lower them after a losing one.

The best practices for monitoring risk in each trade should be followed, and future positions should be estimated taking changes in overall risk into account. retracing the first trading opportunity's backtest. The entry point should be changed to the moment where the deal was no longer valid if any are.

It is best to exit the trade. All other trades should be canceled if no other deals have been made on that position.

This makes keeping records easier, and a shift in the direction of the price makes it easy to spot on the chart when a trade is no longer prioritized.

Trading Psychology

Emotional Control This is widely regarded as the most crucial and difficult to learn trade ability.

There have been numerous books written on this subject, and with good reason. Some pros would go so far as to suggest that a skilled trader is essentially a psychologist, which has a lot of truth to it.

This forex psychology theory builds on the idea that hard work and a good strategy are insufficient to attain trading success.

The losing trader constantly undermines his potential as a top trader by making incorrect and irrational decisions, such as over-trading, choosing poor setups, and over-leveraging because he has an underlying fear of losing what he is essentially feeling.

He is attached to his money. Essentially, he lacks the ability to deal with the psychological anguish of accepting defeat and the dread of being incorrect.

He will convince himself that his emotional actions are not irrational and will frequently blame the trading method. In this scenario, a loser may migrate from system to system in search of a winning strategy.

Obviously, this will just emphasize his failure. A good place to cut losses!

Most traders' first goal is to make a lot of money and be able to do it full-time. The simple truth is that for inexperienced traders, this is not possible to begin with.

This is mainly because new traders are more prone to lack discipline, have poor financial management skills, and be unable to regulate their emotions.

Essentially, you are unprepared to deal with the psychological aspects of trading. These characteristics frequently contribute to overcapitalization and excessive risk-taking, most notably by doubling up or'reopening the deal' when it is not appropriate.

Managing feelings

In the market, it's critical to maintain objectivity and avoid letting your feelings control your decisions. A trader's emotions can destroy them.

Traders who are unable to sense the emotional impact of their actions are among the most successful. A person is capable of making well-considered decisions when he is not influenced by his feelings.

A lot of novices struggle with this. But with time and experience, the trader will learn to manage the different scenarios that arise and cope with the psychological components of trading.

Putting in place mechanical trading systems is one way to assist in this regard. By creating a system with clear guidelines, fear and greed can no longer have any power.

is not following the system. Determining the most likely cause of feelings or actions is another benefit of mechanical systems. This can be explained by contrasting profitable and unsuccessful trades.

The reason behind an emotional reaction can then be identified with more knowledge of the system and how trading is carried out. The result of a deal that happens by accident rather than as a strategy is the most frequent source of an emotional reaction.

In this situation, the trader needs to understand that the method of execution—rather than the outcome—is what matters, and that the system needs to be used often to get past this feeling.

The importance of discipline development For those who have never done it, day trading may appear like a simple way to make money, but the failure rate for day traders is actually rather high.

Within the first year, 90% of traders fail. A lack of discipline is one of the primary causes of the high failure rate among day traders, while there are other contributing aspects as well.

Developing discipline is the key to creating and following a trading plan. Even if you have the best plan in the world, you won't follow it if you lack discipline.

Additionally, discipline will prevent you from taking unwarranted chances or becoming avaricious after you have had a string of profitable trades. What you must do: Being disciplined is a mental state. While some people are more free-spirited, others are more organized and meticulous in their approach.

It may be more difficult for you to acquire discipline if you are a more free-spirited person, but it is still achievable. Discipline might be as easy as creating a routine for those of you who are more impulsive.

You should have specific times of the day when you start and stop trading if you are a full-time trader.

Apart from that, you should schedule particular times of the day to review your transactions, assess the state of the market, and refine your approach.

Additionally, you ought to designate particular days of the week on which you will perform tasks including collecting data and reviewing trade and market data.

Managing losses

Trading also involves handling losses. No matter how much experience a trader has, the inevitable will happen.

Keeping an optimistic outlook while following a methodical approach is a good way to handle losses.

The average amount you can anticipate winning (or losing) for every dollar at stake is known as expectation. It is a helpful method to observe how outcomes may impact trade in the future.

Assume that a trader's victory rate is 60%. His expectation is (0.60 * 100) - (0.40 * 100) = 60 - 40 = $20 if his average winner and loser are both $100. This implies that he can anticipate earning $20 for every $100 risked.

If the trader can double his average win with the same 60% win rate,The revised expectation would be (0.60 * 200) - (0.40 * 50) = 120 - 20 = $40 if he were to cut his average loss in half.

A series of losses might serve as a reality check, which is why the system's anticipation is so crucial.

A trader may believe that everything has gone wrong after a string of losses, even though he could have had a string of profitable trades. However, many traders find it hard to accept this fact.

The trader may stay composed and keep making transactions with an expectation of $40 since he is aware that the long-term trend and probability are in his favor.

The trader might use expectation as a guide to help them make rational judgments by adhering to following the plan with the knowledge that future outcomes should be profitable if the successes are allowed to continue.

Conclusion

Traders employ chart patterns to assess the price's direction and possible range.

Chart patterns like as head and shoulders, triangles, cup and handles, double/triple tops and bottoms, flag pennants, rounded bottoms, and wedges all provide entry opportunities, stop loss levels, and profit target estimations, making them nearly complete strategies.

To trade these patterns as a comprehensive method, traders include them into their trading plan while also determining the appropriate position size for each transaction.

Gaps can be utilized as entry or exit points, depending on whether they indicate a continuance of the trend or a reversal, as well as for analysis. Observing a chart pattern can provide information.